This book is to be returned on or before
the last date stamped below

Tudor Art

Susie Hodge

Heinemann
LIBRARY

First published in Great Britain by Heinemann Library
Halley Court, Jordan Hill, Oxford OX2 8EJ
a division of Reed Educational and Professional Publishing Ltd

OXFORD FLORENCE PRAGUE MADRID ATHENS
MELBOURNE AUCKLAND KUALA LUMPUR SINGAPORE TOKYO
IBADAN NAIROBI KAMPALA JOHANNESBURG GABORONE
PORTSMOUTH NH CHICAGO MEXICO CITY SAO PAULO

© Reed Educational and Professional Publishing Ltd 1997

Produced by Plum Creative
Illustrations by Oxford Illustrators
Printed in Malaysia

01 00 99 98 97
10 9 8 7 6 5 4 3 2 1

ISBN 0 431 05625 0

British Library Cataloguing in Publication Data
Hodge, Susie
    Tudor art. – (Art in history)
    1. Art, British – Juvenile literature 2. Art, Tudor
    Great Britain – Juvenile literature
    I. Title
    709.4'1'09031

Acknowledgements
The publishers would like to thank the following for permission to reproduce photographs:
A F Kersting p26; A K G Photo p14; Ancient Art & Architecture Collection p8; Bridgeman Art Library: Courtesy of The British Library, London p13, Thyssen - Bornemisza Collection p15, Vatican Museums & Galleries, Rome pp10-11, Victoria & Albert Museum p17; Philip Craven Photo Library p25; Fotomas Index p7; Angelo Hornak Library, courtesy of the Dean & Chapter Westminster Abbey p21; Mansell Collection pp9, 12; National Museum & Gallery, Cardiff p4; National Portrait Gallery, London pp16, 19, 28; National Trust Photographic Library pp20, 22, 23, 27; The Royal Collection © Her Majesty the Queen p18; Thetford Museum p29; Westminster Cathedral Library p6.

Cover photograph reproduced with permission of Woburn Abbey, London.

Our thanks to Paul Flux and Jane Shuter for their comments in the preparation of this book.

Cover picture:
The 'Armada' Portrait, about 1588, George Gower (worked as a painter from 1540–96), oil on canvas.

The artist painted this portrait of Queen Elizabeth I by looking at a mask that had been made of her face. It was painted to celebrate the English victory over the Spanish who sent a fleet of ships (the Armada) to overthrow Elizabeth in 1588. The Queen looks flat and doll-like, yet her clothes are detailed and splendid to show her power. The ruff around her neck is of delicate lace and the dress is made from rich fabric covered in expensive gold thread and pearls. The background scenes behind her tell how the Armada was beaten. On the left, the English are sending burning ships to attack the Spanish ships. On the right, the Armada is in a gale. Elizabeth's crown, the chair she sits on and the globe under her right hand show that she ruled England, and England ruled the seas.

CONTENTS

WHAT WAS TUDOR ART?

The Tudor family ruled Britain from 1485–1603. The art of that time shows us what life was like, how ideas developed and how art changed the way some people thought. Most of all, it shows us what people at that time thought of themselves.

Who paid Tudor artists?

Tudor artists needed to sell their work to earn money. They relied on rich people, especially the royal family, for patronage (payment for work). This might explain why the portraits of royalty were more flattering than written descriptions! Also, artists often had to rely on the patronage of the church for more work.

The Tudor Succession, about 1570,
Lucas de Heere (1534–84),
131 x 184 cm, oil on **panel**.

Paintings showing several monarchs were called dynastic paintings. This painting is also an **allegory**. It was painted soon after Elizabeth I became queen. Elizabeth I is on the right, followed by ancient Roman goddesses who symbolized peace and wealth. Edward VI is between Elizabeth I and Henry VIII. On the left are Mary I and her husband, Philip of Spain, followed by Mars, the god of war. Elizabeth I wanted to tell people that she would bring peace and prosperity to the country, while her sister Mary I had brought only trouble.

Who were the Tudors?

Henry Tudor ruled as King Henry VII from 1485 to 1509. When he died his son became Henry VIII (from 1509 to 1547). When Henry VIII died, his son, Edward VI, ruled (from 1547 to 1553). The crown went to Edward VI instead of one of his older sisters because the crown always passed to boys first. Edward VI was only sixteen when he died, and his half-sister **succeeded** him. She was Mary I (queen from 1553 to 1558). Henry VIII's other daughter, Elizabeth I (queen from 1558 to 1603), succeeded Mary I as the last of the Tudors. She never married and did not have any children. When she died the crown passed to her cousin James Stuart, which ended the Tudor age.

The Tudor Rose

The Tudor Rose was designed for Henry VII when he married Elizabeth of York. This marriage ended the wars between the Lancastrians and Yorkists. His rose united the white rose of York with the red rose of Lancaster.

ART AND RELIGION

In 1485 Engalnd was a Catholic country. So were most other countries in Europe. The head of the Catholic Church was the Pope. The Pope was very powerful, he ruled his own country as well as being the head of the Catholic Church everywhere.

Pictures and prayers

Church services were in Latin which most people did not understand. So church walls were painted with scenes from the Bible and other holy images that could be understood. Rich people sometimes bought paintings, statuettes or ornaments for the Church. They believed that this would please God and mean they would go to heaven when they died.

Mary I 'touching the scrofula', 1556, book illustration.

Tudor people believed that their king or queen was chosen by God and so had special powers. Here, Mary I touches a sick person in order to heal her.

Religious changes

Some people began to complain about the Catholic Church. They said that it was too rich and powerful and that services should be in the people's own language. The protesters began new Christian churches, called Protestant churches. In Tudor England many arguments followed between Protestants and Catholics.

Kings, queens and religious problems

When Henry VIII wanted to divorce his first wife, Catherine, and marry his second wife, Anne, the Pope would not allow it. So Henry went against the Pope and made himself the Head of the Church in England. Edward VI believed in Protestant ideas, but after him came Mary I who was a Catholic. Elizabeth I was a Protestant but she was understanding about other religions.

How art was affected

Catholics and Protestants believed that the way they worshipped God would make a difference as to whether they went to heaven or hell when they died. People from both churches were prepared to die for their beliefs. Wars were fought and art was affected. Protestant churches did not want wall paintings because their services could be understood. Nor did they want expensive statues or ornaments.

Bishop's Bible, 1572, Franciscus Hogenburg (1540–90), 280 x 187 mm, frontispiece.

This is a page from an English Bible that was printed during Elizabeth I's reign (Elizabeth was a Protestant).

MATERIALS AND METHODS

Tudor artists were among the lowest paid workers. They belonged to **guilds** which had strict rules about prices and ways of working. Guild members who broke the rules were fined. Artists could only set themselves up in business if they were members. Boys who wanted to be artists had to become **apprentices** first and learn in the workshop of a master artist or craftsman.

After seven years each apprentice produced a 'masterpiece' to show that he had done well. Then, if he could pay the large fee needed to become a master in the guild, he could set up a business on his own. If he was too poor he had to become a journeyman. Journeymen were hired and paid by the day.

Artist at work, 1568, Jost Amman (1539–91), 70 x 90 cm, woodcut.

This shows an artist painting at an easel. His apprentice is busy in the background.

Ideas and inventions

At the start of Tudor times, ink made from nut juice was being used in Europe. **Pastels** were being used during the period of Elizabeth I's reign. The first pencil was made in 1565 in Switzerland (charcoal had been used before).

Oil paints were also becoming popular. Before, paint had been made by adding egg or wax to dry **pigments** to make a paste. Then a Flemish artist, Jan van Eyck, began mixing walnut or linseed oil with his pigments instead.

The new oil paint dried slowly, so artists could correct their work more easily. Paintbrushes were made by tying hairs around a stick with waxed thread. Artists began to use **canvas** to paint on instead of wood. Canvas was light and could be rolled up to carry easily.

With the invention of the printing press came an increase in the number of books. This meant that new ideas reached people more easily. It also meant that more artists were needed to produce illustrations.

Book Printing, 1568, Jost Amman (1539–91), 70 x 90 cm, woodcut.

This shows a printer's workshop. The men at the back set each word, letter by letter, into a wooden frame which is the size of a page. At the front, one man puts ink on to the type; the other puts the paper in place.

THE REBIRTH OF ART

Tudor art was slowly changed by events taking place in the rest of Europe, especially in Italy and Flanders (Flanders is now part of Belgium and France). People were taking a new interest in the art, **architecture**, science and literature of ancient Greek and Roman times. Artists also studied mathematics and the human body to make their work look realistic and three-dimensional. This period of time was named the **Renaissance**, which means 'rebirth'. It continued for nearly 200 years.

A brilliant man

Leonardo da Vinci (1452–1519) was a Renaissance artist, scientist and engineer. He designed flying machines and submarines long before they were invented. He carefully studied how things were constructed and made thousands of drawings and plans. He wrote down his discoveries in secret 'back-to-front' writing.

*The School of Athens, about 1510–12, Raphael (1483–1520), width at its base 7.7 m; **fresco**.*

*Raphael admired both Leonardo and Michelangelo. His brilliantly coloured fresco (one of several he painted for the Pope) represents the great thinkers of ancient Greece. Raphael studied real people including himself and his friends in the painting. The life-sized, solid looking figures are arranged in a perfectly balanced **composition**. Raphael has also used new **perspective** techniques to show space and distance.*

Michelangelo

Michelangelo Buonarroti was another artist who worked on many different forms of art. He was a painter, sculptor, architect and poet. He is particularly famous for his sculpture and for his fresco on the ceiling of the Sistine Chapel in Rome.

Lifelike pictures

Renaissance art was full of lifelike details. It was very different to the art completed before the Renaissance, which had become much less realistic. The ideas of the Renaissance were passed on through books and by travellers. But travel was slow and difficult, so it took a long time for the ideas to spread.

The Sistine Chapel's ceiling in Rome, 1508–12, Michelangelo (1475–1564), fresco.

Michelangelo took four years to paint the whole ceiling. While painting the ceiling he lay flat on his back on wooden scaffolding, 20 metres above the ground. The result of his work is fantastic. The 300 figures in the painting seem to spring out of the ceiling, bringing the Bible to life for everyone who sees it. It is one of the world's greatest masterpieces.

ART AND BOOKS

The invention of **movable type** in 1447 made printing books even easier. Books helped to spread new ideas and knowledge. Most early printed books were religious.

The Burnyng of Cranmer, from Foxe's 'Book of Martyrs', 1563, 330 x 185 mm woodcut.

*This is a woodcut from a famous book, showing Protestant **martyrs** being burned for refusing to become Catholics. Some of the book's pictures are quite gruesome. Cranmer was the Archbishop of Canterbury. Catholics burnt him at the stake because he was a Protestant. You can see him stretching his hand into the flame, saying 'Lord receive my Spirite'. Tudor spelling was different to ours – Frier John was a monk, not a cook!*

Printing pictures

Book illustrations were made by the ancient method of woodcut. First a back-to-front picture was cut into a block of wood and then covered with ink, made of oil and soot. When paper was pressed on to the block, a print appeared the right way round. Some prints were very detailed and tiny tools were needed to cut them. Woodcuts were cheap, easy to produce and thousands of copies of a picture could be printed from one block.

*This was for the front of a book of poems by Charles, the Duke of Orleans in France. The **illuminated** letter 'D' is an example of how books were illustrated before printing had been invented.*

The painting shows the Duke when he was imprisoned in the Tower of London. He is shown at the window of the White Tower, riding through an arch in the tower on the left and also writing a letter at a desk. The Duke was released in 1440, but we know the picture was painted about sixty years later because the London buildings are painted as they looked in 1500.

Flat pictures

Many of the artists who made woodcuts did not know about the ideas of the **Renaissance** artists and the use of **perspective**. Their pictures seem much flatter. Many of the woodcut artists were not as skilled as Renaissance artists.

Painted books

Coloured pictures like this painting of London could not be printed like they can today. Each one had to painted by hand, so few Tudor books contained coloured pictures.

TUDOR PORTRAITS

Henry VIII was broad-shouldered, with red hair, a long nose and a small mouth. How do we know this? Because we have **portraits** of the king. The most well-known paintings from Tudor times were portraits commissioned, or ordered, by the rich and powerful.

No smiling

The nobility ordered portraits to show their power. Good portrait painters showed people in dark colours with serious expressions, in family groups or alone. One of the most famous portrait painters of Tudor times was Hans Holbein.

Hans Holbein the Younger (1497–1543)

German-born Hans Holbein was the son of a painter. He trained in his father's studio and later moved to Switzerland. There he designed woodcuts. He painted portraits and religious subjects. In 1532 he moved to England and soon found work painting portraits of rich merchants and courtiers. Henry VIII asked Holbein to paint members of the royal household and his fame spread. Holbein died in London of the plague in 1543.

Henry VIII, 1536, Hans Holbein (1497–1543), 28 x 19 cm, oil and **tempera** on oak panel.

The black background symbolizes power. The king is looking at the viewer and almost fills the frame. He seems greater than us. His eyes and mouth are stern; his clothes and magnificent jewellery look expensive. This powerful but small portrait was painted in the year that Henry's first wife died, his second wife was beheaded, and he married his third!

Holbein painted this when he first arrived in London. Georg was a merchant. You can see his belongings all around him, including his scales and weights and the wax seals for marking documents. Unlike most English artists, Holbein had seen Italian **Renaissance** paintings and had learned about **composition**, balance and how to observe everything closely. See how Georg's eyes look straight at you even though his body is slightly turned away.

Holbein captured every sitter's personality. People were amazed at how lifelike his subjects looked. Many other artists tried to copy Holbein, but he is still one of the greatest portrait painters in history.

A GREAT QUEEN

Elizabeth I lived from 1533 to 1603. During her life many **portraits** were painted of her, but some did not show what she really looked like. There are many reasons for this. For example, she did not like the idea of growing old and wanted to appear young, even later in life.

Also, she wanted her portraits to influence how people felt about her. She had control over her portrait painters. She sent her favourite artists on tours to far away parts of the country. This meant the artists could not see what she really looked like.

Elizabeth I (The 'Ditchley' Portrait), 1592, Marcus Geeraerts the Younger (1561–1636), 241.3 x 152.4 cm, oil on canvas.

This full-length portrait has Elizabeth standing astride the world. Her feet are on England, by Ditchley, where an entertainment had been given in her honour. The sun represents her glory and the thunder her power.

The picture is detailed but flat-looking. For once the Queen has not been made to look young. As a forceful figure towering over her country she has been made to look wise and great. She is wearing magnificent clothes and jewels to show her wealth and power.

Miniatures

Miniatures were tiny portraits that became particularly popular during Tudor times. Nicholas Hilliard (1547–1619) was the son of a goldsmith who became chief portrait painter to the queen in 1584. He also painted beautiful miniatures in the tradition of monks' **illuminated manuscripts**.

How Hilliard made miniatures

First he would cut a playing card into an oval shape and cover it with **vellum**. Next he would coat the vellum with flesh-coloured paint.

He would draw the picture lightly with a pencil and then build up the details gradually, with thin layers of paint and real gold leaf. Hilliard always used clear, brilliant colours, grinding them himself on a crystal block and mixing them with distilled water and **gum arabic**.

You could try making your own miniature with card and paints.

Elizabeth I, 1572, Nicholas Hilliard (1547–1619), 5 x 4.5 cm, oil on vellum.

Hilliard always painted Elizabeth I in a clear light with no shadows. His miniatures looked like jewels and were often worn as such.

(Actual size)

STORY-TELLING PICTURES

At the beginning of the Tudor period only Royal or noble homes had paintings. Most of these were **portraits** of people in the family. By the end of the Tudor period artists were painting family portraits for more people. They were also painting many other things, from decorations for **pageants** and **masques**, to wooden panelling in houses. Occasionally artists were asked to paint a picture that told a story.

The Field of the Cloth of Gold, 1520, artist unknown, 168 x 347 cm, oil on panel.

This told the story of Henry VIII's meeting with French king, Francis I, in 1520 in France. The meeting became known as the 'Field of the Cloth of Gold' because so much gold cloth was used in the tents and decorations. The painting features Henry VIII several times. In the front he rides with his attendants with a dragon firework flying above. Towards the back both kings and their queens are watching the jousting from beside a tent.

Sir Henry Unton, 1596, artist unknown, 163 x 74 cm, oil on panel.

Sir Henry Unton was a well-to-do gentleman, landowner, soldier, MP and the queen's ambassador to France during Elizabeth I's reign. At his widow's request, his life was recorded in this large painting. Find him in his study and at a musical banquet with his wife. Other scenes show his mother; Unton studying at Oxford; travelling in Venice, the Low Countries and France; on his sick-bed; his body being carried back to England; the funeral procession. Outside his house poor people are mourning his death.

This type of story-telling painting was unusual. Maps were more likely to be hung on walls than pictures, and portraits were the most popular paintings.

Art for the rich

Only the rich could afford paintings, so poor people were rarely shown in them.

Paint palette

Tudor artists made paint from grinding natural materials. Charcoal produced black; earth gave browns; chalk produced white. The lapis lazuli stone gave bright blue; copper produced green; a red rock, red; lead-tin, yellow. Sometimes real gold was used, too.

19

STYLES IN SCULPTURE

Wealthy people paid artists to make paintings of themselves and their families to show how important they were. They also paid sculptors to carve grand tombs for when they died. Tomb sculpture changed during the period just as **portrait** painting did. It took on the more realistic style of the **Renaissance**.

Slow changes

By the 1500s, sculptors had begun to copy decorative details from Renaissance artists, but they missed the basic idea of making the human form realistic. Although the tombs were detailed, the figures in them looked stiff and unnatural. Henry VIII employed an Italian sculptor, who had trained with Michelangelo, to create his parents' tomb.

Tomb of William Sharington.

William Sharington died in 1553. The sculptor of his tomb carved detailed and precise decorations making sure that each side matched the other. The tomb is made of **marble, alabaster** *and expensive imported materials. Notice the little figures, the crests and the fancy decorations. This skilful work was in demand. Even the dead had to look fashionable!*

The Renaissance reaches Britain

Henry VII's tomb stands out not just because Torrigiano was a great artist, but because of how he worked. The statues' positions, their faces and clothes are more lifelike and natural-looking than any other sculpture being produced in Britain at the time.

Other work for sculptors

Sculptors were not encouraged to create masterpieces like the Renaissance artists. Although Henry VIII paid for this tomb he did not seem to have been interested in sculpture as decorative art. What the king wanted (or did not want) set the fashion so few other people wanted decorative sculpture either.

Tombs were almost the only way sculptors could earn money and the **patrons** wanted them to look impressive, not realistic.

*Henry VII's tomb in Westminster Abbey, 1512–18, Pietro Torrigiano (1472–1528), **gilt**, **bronze**, black and white marble.*

Torrigiano came to England from 1511 to 1522. He worked on the two life-size statues of Henry VII and his wife, Elizabeth of York, for four years.

DECORATIVE CARVINGS

Masons, woodcarvers and stonecarvers decorated buildings, inside and out, with imaginative carvings. The work was valued by how well the materials were used. There were strict **guild** rules about the materials that should be used. Artists usually worked on the spot, which sometimes meant being high on a roof or beside a window. They carved the fine details by hand using metal tools like **chisels** and **files**. They signed their work by carving marks or faces into the wood or stone.

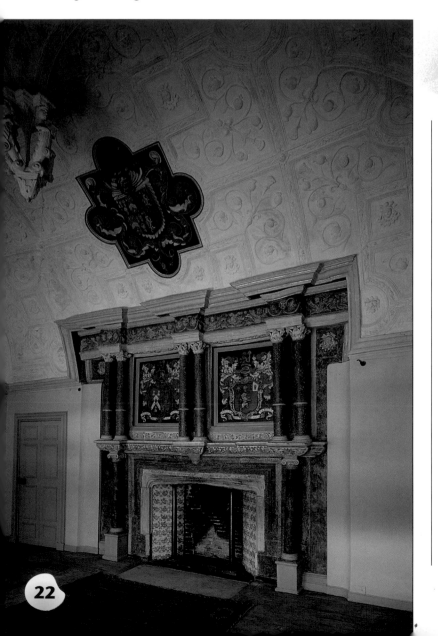

Chimney piece from Canons Ashby, Northamptonshire, originally made in about 1590, plaster, brick and iron.

Fires were the only form of heating in Tudor times. Chimneys replaced simple smoke holes in the roof. This meant large fireplaces became an important part of each room. This impressive looking fireplace was made out of plaster and painted to look like **marble**, with gold leaf and other coloured paints. The crests were painted in later (in about 1634) and put on top of original oval shaped painted panels. The blue tiles were also added much later. Designs such as flowers, animals, fruit, leaves and scrolls were common features on grand Tudor fireplaces. Small carved figures began to replace the plainer pillars and columns during Elizabeth's reign.

Panels and patterns

Wallpaper was rare so panelling was popular in Tudor homes and churches. This helped to make the rooms warmer but made them dark. Small squares of wood or panels were fixed to the walls with a grid of wooden strips in front. Patterns were carved into the panels. Sometimes panels were painted to add colour to the room.

Decorations everywhere

Outside walls were decorated mainly around the windows, doors, chimneys and **buttresses**, with carved animals, angels and **gargoyles**. The Tudor Rose, designed for Henry VII, was used a lot, so were **fleur-de-lys**, crinkled ribbons and vines. Ceilings were decorated with complicated plaster patterns. Even rainwater pipes and door hinges were carved into decorative shapes.

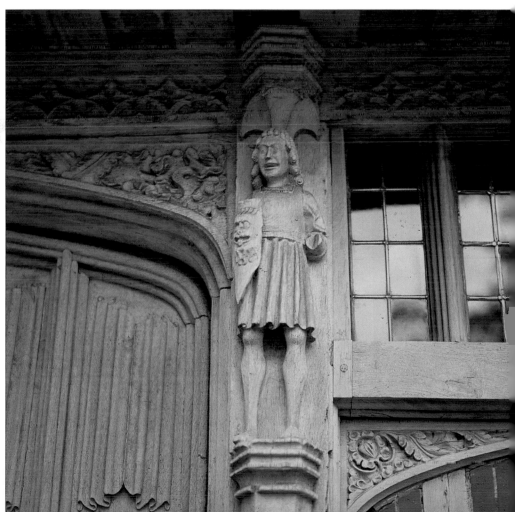

Paycocke's House, Coggleshaw, Essex, 1505, door and window carving, oak.

In 1505, a wealthy wool merchant had this house built as a wedding present to his son, Thomas Paycocke. There is a lot of carving on both the inside and outside of the house. This man and the leaves have been carved in wood to match other details around the outside of the house.

TUDOR BUILDINGS

Great improvements were made to houses during Tudor times. **Architecture** developed as new houses were built. Master **masons** were the chief builders. They designed the buildings and told the other craftsmen (masons, stonecarvers, woodcarvers, glassmakers and carpenters) what to do.

As well as houses, more schools, colleges, universities and places to care for the poor were built all over the country. Master masons used materials that were found locally, but stone, red brick and terracotta became particularly popular.

Make a model Tudor house

Materials:
different sized cardboard boxes

card	paper
scissors	glue
sticky tape	ruler
pencil	paint or felt-tipped pens

1 Stack your boxes together to make up the shape of a house. Glue or tape them into position and paint them white. Shape the top of the house like a roof.

2 Cut out a door. Draw or paint windows on paper rectangles and stick them on.

3 Using a ruler draw the wooden frame. Paint or colour it dark brown or black. Fold some card for the roof. Paint it reddish-brown to look like terracotta (clay) tiles or a yellow-brown to look like straw thatch. Stick it on the house.

How houses were built

Many well-off people had half-timbered houses. They had a stone or brick base to stop dampness from damaging the walls. A wooden frame was built on top, called wattle, and the gaps in between were filled with daub, which could be made with mud, chopped straw and manure. Plaster was put over the daub. Instead of holes in the roof to let out smoke, proper brick chimneys were built. This was a great improvement because before houses were filled with smoke.

Many of these houses had glass windows of small diamond-shapes, fixed together with lead strips. Glass was expensive. If people could not afford glass, they used pieces of polished horn. Some houses had no upstairs rooms, just high ceilings. Others had upstairs rooms that stuck out which were called jetties. These made upstairs rooms bigger and protected downstairs rooms from bad weather.

Almshouses, Windsor Castle.

Well-off people left money in their wills for almshouses to be built, to give poor people somewhere to live.

CASTLES AND COURTS

The Tudors brought peace to England after many years of fighting. Great homes no longer had to be defended against attack. So people built grand mansions and manor houses which were designed to be comfortable homes and not fortresses.

Hampton Court Palace, Surrey, building began 1514, master mason Henry Redman (died 1528), red brick.

This was first built for Cardinal Wolsey, but he gave it to Henry VIII in 1529. It was made almost entirely of rose-red bricks. Craftsmen from several countries worked on the magnificent building, carving detailed decorations both inside and out.

Styled to impress

Rich Tudors wanted impressive homes, so master **masons** experimented with new styles. They mixed Italian **Renaissance** designs with English ideas and made buildings that looked as magnificent as ancient castles but were more comfortable. Stone was the most common building material, but red brick became popular too. Because glass was expensive, large windows became a symbol of wealth, as were tall decorated chimneys. Windows were sometimes filled with **stained glass**. They looked like transparent oil paintings.

Stained glass window, from the chapel at The Vyne, Northamptonshire, about 1520, glass and lead.

This stained glass window shows Catherine of Aragon, Henry VIII's first wife, kneeling. The rich colours are clear, yet the picture is detailed. The textures of the materials and pillars have been painted to look realistic. Notice the little dog curled up asleep and the gentle landscape in the background. Stained glass windows were a great luxury in Tudor times.

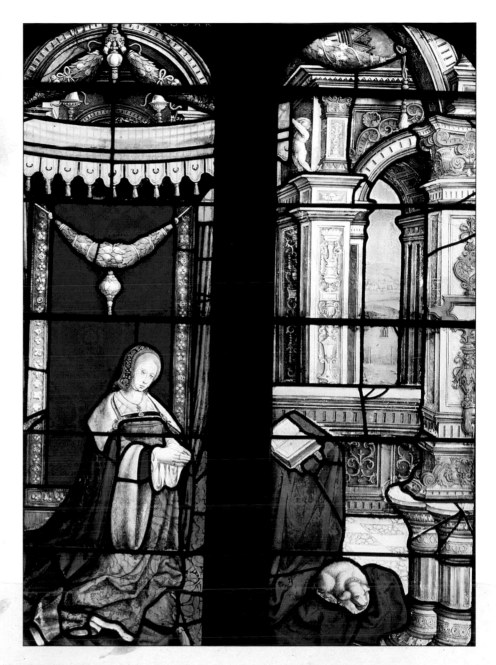

How stained glass windows were made

First an artist drew the design on a whitewash-coated table. Then the shapes, sizes, positions and colours of the pieces of glass were marked on the table. A heated iron tool was used to cut the glass to the right shapes. Any rough edges were smoothed. The pieces of glass were then laid on the table over the design.

The artist painted on any details with special paint. Next, the glass pieces were laid out on an iron plate, covered with ashes and heated in a **kiln**. This made the paint stick to the glass. After the glass had cooled, lead was moulded round each piece of glass and the picture was put together like a jigsaw.

UNDERSTANDING TUDOR ART

During the Tudor age artists had to follow accepted rules. They could only use certain materials and paint or sculpt traditional subjects. Changes did not happen as often or as quickly as they do today. Yet the achievements, inventions and discoveries made during Tudor times meant that changes and developments did occur in art, too. Religious changes forced artists to think of new ideas. **Renaissance** art that amazed the rest of Europe came late to England, bringing a style of its own when it did. New methods and equipment gave artists the chance to develop new skills.

Prince Edward, 1546, William Scrotts, (worked from 1537–53) 42.5 x 160 cm, oil on panel.

This curious picture has a curious name. It is called anamorphosis, a Greek word that means 'transform'. Close your right eye, and hold the right-hand side of the picture close to your left eye. Now you can see the face and background properly.

Curious art

Wealthy people ordered colourful wall-hangings, panel paintings or **portraits** for their homes to impress other people. Some people bought carpets from foreign lands, but not to put on the floors. Look again at Holbein's portrait of Georg Gisze on page 14. Rich people put their carpets on tables.

Three years after Holbein died, William Scrotts became King's Painter to Henry VIII. He had picked up many ideas from Holbein and he knew all the latest fashions in court painting. As well as several portraits of Henry VIII's family, Scrotts painted an unusual picture of Prince Edward.

SYMONDS of
Cº. Norfolk.

Mr Symonds of Norfolk, 1595–1600, artist unknown 76 x 96.5 cm, oil on panel.

This is a fine example of how ordinary gentlemen began to commission portraits of themselves. We can see that Mr Symonds was a gentleman because there is a hooded falcon on his hand. Only gentlemen went hawking. Also, he probably owned the ploughed fields behind him. But we know that the artist was not too expensive as he was not very skilled. The horse looks like a rocking horse with all its legs apart at once, and Mr Symonds is too large for his horse. The most skilful artists charged a lot of money – probably more than Mr Symonds could afford.

TIMELINE

GLOSSARY

alabaster translucent (slightly see-through) creamy-white stone

allegory a picture of something that is being used to mean something else

apprentices young people who learn a trade or craft under the direction of a skilled worker

architecture the design and construction of buildings

bronze brownish-gold metal; made of a mixture of copper and tin

buttresses thick stone or brick pillars built against the outside of a wall to strengthen and support it

canvas strong woven cloth, traditionally made of hemp or linen

chisels metal tools with sharp edges used for carving

composition the arrangement of a piece of art

easel a stand used to support a painting

files metal tools with a rough surface to smooth the edges of carvings

Fleur-de-lys a stylised design of a lily with three petals joined together at the bottom

fresco a wall painting made on damp, fresh plaster (fresco means 'fresh' in Italian)

gargoyles stone spouts to carry water off a roof, and often carved to look like monsters

gilt gold-like metal or a metal covered thinly with gold

guilds societies of craftsmen who all do the same job. They have to pay to join and must obey guild rules.

gum arabic glue-like gum

illuminated (manuscripts) decorated handwritten books or documents, usually in gold, silver and brilliant colours

kiln an extremely hot oven used to heat materials such as clay or pottery.

marble a hard rock that can be polished to a shine. It comes in all sorts of colours, some with swirly patterns.

martyr a person who is killed for their religious beliefs

masques dances or plays where the performers wear masks

mason someone who cuts, shapes and builds in stone and brick

movable type the first form of printing using metal letters, invented in Germany by Johann Gutenberg in 1455

pageants/pageantry colourful parades of people

pastels soft, coloured chalks (from the Italian word pasta, meaning paste)

patrons people who buy artists' work

perspective a way of showing space or distance on a flat surface

pigment coloured powder that gives paint its colour

portrait a picture of a real person or animal

Renaissance the word means 'rebirth' and describes the new interest in classical art and learning. The Renaissance lasted from about 1400 to about 1520.

stained glass pieces of coloured glass held in place by strips of lead to make a picture

succeeded took a person's place after they had died

tempera pigment mixed with egg yolk, making a quick-drying paint

vellum fine parchment, like a smooth paper

INDEX

Numbers in plain type (24) refer to the text.
Numbers in bold type (**28**) refer to an illustration.